Crystal Magic

2024

WEEKLY PLANNER

JULY 2023 – DECEMBER 2024

ROCK
POINT

2024 Year at a Glance

JANUARY

S	M	T	W	T	F	S
	1	2	3	4	5	6
7	8	9	10	11	12	13
14	15	16	17	18	19	20
21	22	23	24	25	26	27
28	29	30	31			

FEBRUARY

S	M	T	W	T	F	S
				1	2	3
4	5	6	7	8	9	10
11	12	13	14	15	16	17
18	19	20	21	22	23	24
25	26	27	28	29		

MARCH

S	M	T	W	T	F	S
					1	2
3	4	5	6	7	8	9
10	11	12	13	14	15	16
17	18	19	20	21	22	23
24	25	26	27	28	29	30
31						

APRIL

S	M	T	W	T	F	S
	1	2	3	4	5	6
7	8	9	10	11	12	13
14	15	16	17	18	19	20
21	22	23	24	25	26	27
28	29	30				

MAY

S	M	T	W	T	F	S
			1	2	3	4
5	6	7	8	9	10	11
12	13	14	15	16	17	18
19	20	21	22	23	24	25
26	27	28	29	30	31	

JUNE

S	M	T	W	T	F	S
						1
2	3	4	5	6	7	8
9	10	11	12	13	14	15
16	17	18	19	20	21	22
23	24	25	26	27	28	29
30						

JULY

S	M	T	W	T	F	S
	1	2	3	4	5	6
7	8	9	10	11	12	13
14	15	16	17	18	19	20
21	22	23	24	25	26	27
28	29	30	31			

AUGUST

S	M	T	W	T	F	S
				1	2	3
4	5	6	7	8	9	10
11	12	13	14	15	16	17
18	19	20	21	22	23	24
25	26	27	28	29	30	31

SEPTEMBER

S	M	T	W	T	F	S
1	2	3	4	5	6	7
8	9	10	11	12	13	14
15	16	17	18	19	20	21
22	23	24	25	26	27	28
29	30					

OCTOBER

S	M	T	W	T	F	S
		1	2	3	4	5
6	7	8	9	10	11	12
13	14	15	16	17	18	19
20	21	22	23	24	25	26
27	28	29	30	31		

NOVEMBER

S	M	T	W	T	F	S
					1	2
3	4	5	6	7	8	9
10	11	12	13	14	15	16
17	18	19	20	21	22	23
24	25	26	27	28	29	30

DECEMBER

S	M	T	W	T	F	S
1	2	3	4	5	6	7
8	9	10	11	12	13	14
15	16	17	18	19	20	21
22	23	24	25	26	27	28
29	30	31				

2025 Year at a Glance

JANUARY

S	M	T	W	T	F	S
			1	2	3	4
5	6	7	8	9	10	11
12	13	14	15	16	17	18
19	20	21	22	23	24	25
26	27	28	29	30	31	

FEBRUARY

S	M	T	W	T	F	S
						1
2	3	4	5	6	7	8
9	10	11	12	13	14	15
16	17	18	19	20	21	22
23	24	25	26	27	28	

MARCH

S	M	T	W	T	F	S
						1
2	3	4	5	6	7	8
9	10	11	12	13	14	15
16	17	18	19	20	21	22
23	24	25	26	27	28	29
30	31					

APRIL

S	M	T	W	T	F	S
		1	2	3	4	5
6	7	8	9	10	11	12
13	14	15	16	17	18	19
20	21	22	23	24	25	26
27	28	29	30			

MAY

S	M	T	W	T	F	S
				1	2	3
4	5	6	7	8	9	10
11	12	13	14	15	16	17
18	19	20	21	22	23	24
25	26	27	28	29	30	31

JUNE

S	M	T	W	T	F	S
1	2	3	4	5	6	7
8	9	10	11	12	13	14
15	16	17	18	19	20	21
22	23	24	25	26	27	28
29	30					

JULY

S	M	T	W	T	F	S
		1	2	3	4	5
6	7	8	9	10	11	12
13	14	15	16	17	18	19
20	21	22	23	24	25	26
27	28	29	30	31		

AUGUST

S	M	T	W	T	F	S
					1	2
3	4	5	6	7	8	9
10	11	12	13	14	15	16
17	18	19	20	21	22	23
24	25	26	27	28	29	30
31						

SEPTEMBER

S	M	T	W	T	F	S
	1	2	3	4	5	6
7	8	9	10	11	12	13
14	15	16	17	18	19	20
21	22	23	24	25	26	27
28	29	30				

OCTOBER

S	M	T	W	T	F	S
			1	2	3	4
5	6	7	8	9	10	11
12	13	14	15	16	17	18
19	20	21	22	23	24	25
26	27	28	29	30	31	

NOVEMBER

S	M	T	W	T	F	S
						1
2	3	4	5	6	7	8
9	10	11	12	13	14	15
16	17	18	19	20	21	22
23	24	25	26	27	28	29
30						

DECEMBER

S	M	T	W	T	F	S
	1	2	3	4	5	6
7	8	9	10	11	12	13
14	15	16	17	18	19	20
21	22	23	24	25	26	27
28	29	30	31			

BIRTHSTONES BY MONTH

January
Garnet

April
Diamond

February
Amethyst

May
Emerald

March
Aquamarine

June
Pearl

July
Ruby

October
Opal

August
Peridot

November
Topaz

September
Sapphire

December
Turquoise

JULY 2023

NOTES	SUNDAY	MONDAY	TUESDAY
		2 ○	3	4
				INDEPENDENCE DAY (US)
	9 ☽	10	11
	16 ●	17	18
	23	24 ☾	25
	30	31	

JULY 2023

WEDNESDAY	THURSDAY	FRIDAY	SATURDAY
			1 CANADA DAY (CAN)
5	6	7	8
12	13	14	15
19	20	21	22
26	27	28	29

CITRINE

Citrine, of the quartz family, radiates sunny optimism. This yellow-hued stone is warming, nurturing, and energizing. It uplifts and bursts with life. Citrine can help clarify your thoughts, especially when seeking new paths. It is a restful stone and good to keep nearby when concentration is required or the creative juices are flowing. Natural citrine is rare and well worth the search, but abundantly available as a heat-treated variety of amethyst or smoky quartz. It instills optimism and attracts prosperity, earning it the nickname "merchant's stone."

 Magical force: Citrine manifests abundance and, in turn, increases generosity—sharing wealth brings wealth. Its optimistic nature instills joy and confidence that what you desire can be yours.

 Chakra correspondence: *Solar plexus*—clears the way for health-promoting energies to flow freely through your body.

June / July

MONDAY (JUNE)

26

TUESDAY (JUNE)

27

WEDNESDAY (JUNE)

28

THURSDAY (JUNE)

29

FRIDAY (JUNE)

30

SATURDAY CANADA DAY (CAN)

1

SUNDAY

2

July 2023

MONDAY ○

3

TUESDAY INDEPENDENCE DAY (US)

4

WEDNESDAY

5

THURSDAY

6

FRIDAY

7

SATURDAY

8

SUNDAY

9

RUBY

*Ruby's glorious red color symbolizes
love and passion and promotes energy,
sensuality, and vitality.*

July 2023

10

TUESDAY

11

WEDNESDAY

12

THURSDAY

13

FRIDAY

14

SATURDAY

15

SUNDAY

16

I see the world through rose-colored glasses—with positive intent, love, and compassion for all.

July 2023

MONDAY

17

TUESDAY

18

WEDNESDAY

19

THURSDAY

20

FRIDAY

21

SATURDAY

22

SUNDAY

23

*The crystal gently reflects what's
in your heart so you may see its
messages more clearly.*

July 2023

MONDAY 24

TUESDAY 25

WEDNESDAY 26

THURSDAY 27

FRIDAY

28

SATURDAY

29

SUNDAY

30

I speak with truth. I hear with truth. I act with truth. I love with truth. I trust the Universe and its plan for me.

August

RITUAL

ᴄ· Bath for Patience ·ᴐ

Patience is a virtue and a transcendent type of love, so when you feel like your fuse is a little short, turn to this ritual bath and rose quartz to open your heart.

Gather together the following items:

- At least 1 turquoise crystal for calm
- At least 6 rose quartz crystals, as this is the number of harmony
- 1 blue candle for serenity of the heart
- 6 drops each of essential oils of lavender, chamomile, and rose
- At least 6 rose petals, dried or fresh

1. Dim the lights and light your candle on a heat-safe surface.
2. To a warm bath add your essential oils.
3. Stir the water widdershins (counterclockwise) while envisioning all of the properties of the oils infusing the water.
4. Next, add your rose quartz and turquoise crystals either directly to the water or lining the bathtub ledge near you. Continue to stir widdershins while you envision the water infused with love and self-forgiveness.
5. Sprinkle your rose petals across the top of the water to bring gratitude, grace, and joy.
6. As you climb into the bath, say the following spell quietly or aloud:

These crystals, grown

through time and stress,

prove life does shape us to our best.

These oils bring peace to my heart

and my days, a little patience returns

threefold in endless ways.

AUGUST 2023

| | | | ○ 1 |
| 6 | 7 | ☽ 8 |

SUMMER BANK HOLIDAY
(UK-SCT)

| 13 | 14 | 15 |

| 20 | 21 | 22 |

| 27 | 28 | 29 |

SUMMER BANK HOLIDAY
(UK-ENG / NIR / WAL)

AUGUST 2023

WEDNESDAY	THURSDAY	FRIDAY	SATURDAY
2	3	4	5
9	10	11	12
● 16	17	18	19
23	☾ 24	25	26
○ 30	31		

ROSE QUARTZ

If you listen carefully, you may hear the heartbeat of the Universe in this stone of love. This pink-hued stone, a form of quartz, is a nurturing stone offered by Mother Earth as her expression of unconditional love. Rose quartz beads found in Iraq can be dated back as far as 7000 BCE, and were, perhaps, used as talismans. Its energies can help heal emotional trauma, ease anxiety, release jealousy, mend a forsaken heart, and clear away anything negative that prevents the sending or receiving of love.

Magical force: Rose quartz has a high vibration but a gentle energy that complements meditation, especially if working to soothe angry emotions. Use it in spellwork to attract love or in a ritual bath to add an aura of irresistibility to the love vibes you emanate. As part of a candle magic ritual, it can help send loving energies into the world when it's hurting and needs to be healed.

Chakra correspondence: *Heart*—heals any wounds or pain stored there and opens one up to the healing powers of empathy and compassion, restoring the heart's ability to give and receive love.

July / August

MONDAY (JULY)

31

TUESDAY ○

1

WEDNESDAY

2

THURSDAY

3

FRIDAY

4

SATURDAY

5

SUNDAY

6

August 2023

TUESDAY   8

WEDNESDAY   9

THURSDAY   10

FRIDAY 11

SATURDAY 12

SUNDAY 13

PERIDOT

A symbol of strength, peridot ushers in prosperity and peace.

August 2023

MONDAY

14

TUESDAY

15

WEDNESDAY ●

16

THURSDAY

17

FRIDAY

18

SATURDAY

19

SUNDAY

20

I move in harmony with the Universe
as I seek to manifest a life of grace and joy.

August 2023

FRIDAY

25

SATURDAY

26

SUNDAY

27

Acknowledge what's around you and cultivate a grateful heart as you work toward your desired goals.

September

RITUAL

⌁·Meditation for Confidence·⌁

That self-possessed feeling that one is in control, has what it takes, and all will work out right takes us far in the world. Yet, we often struggle to hold onto it in the moments we need it most. For those times when you need an extra dose of confidence, whether in work, romantic situations, or when stepping out of your comfort zone, do this meditation ritual to strengthen your aura.

Gather the following:

- Back onlyx crystal
- Meditative music (optional)
- Sage-infused spray
- A pen and paper

1. If using, put on your meditative music.
2. Cleanse your space with the sage-infused spray and clear all clutter.
3. Settle in your space and place the black onyx crystal in front of you.
4. Write down all your positive qualities, especially anything you've been told by others.
5. When you're finished, read the list over and over until you have it memorized.
6. Once you've memorized the list and affirmed them in yourself, say the following spell:

I am the good others see in me.

I am the good I see in myself.

Deep beneath the surface lies

the strength to face what life does ask.

I'm doubly equal to the task.

SEPTEMBER 2023

NOTES	SUNDAY	MONDAY	TUESDAY
	3	4	5
	FATHER'S DAY (AUS / NZ)	LABOR DAY (US) LABOUR DAY (CAN)	
	10	11	12
	GRANDPARENTS' DAY (US)	PATRIOT DAY (US)	
	17	18	19
	24	25	26
	YOM KIPPUR (BEGINS AT SUNDOWN)		

SEPTEMBER 2023

WEDNESDAY	THURSDAY	FRIDAY	SATURDAY
		1	2
6	7	8	9
13	14	15	16
		ROSH HASHANAH (BEGINS AT SUNDOWN) FIRST DAY OF NATIONAL HISPANIC HERITAGE MONTH	
20	21	22	23
			FALL EQUINOX
27	28	29	30
		SUKKOT (BEGINS AT SUNDOWN)	

BLACK ONYX

An ancient stone, onyx is a type of chalcedony, and its use dates back to some of the earliest civilizations. It did experience a bit of a reputation as a bad luck stone, but that was often just in the eye of the beholder. Black onyx is a powerful protective stone, giving its owner confidence, strength, and stamina. Because black, as a color, absorbs all the light, it's thought that this quality means black onyx has absorbed all the secrets of the Earth from which it is born. Its power, though, can also be one of letting go.

Magical force: Onyx fosters self-confidence and self-control, and affords protection while taking action. Onyx will absorb your intentions and remind you of the goals you're working to manifest; it helps ideas take root. Placed in a crystal grid, it emanates protection while absorbing negative energy. It is magnificent for scrying. Do not fear the dark: when working with black onyx, you'll feel the wonder of the night sky and its infinite possibilities.

Chakra correspondence: *Root*—grounds you in self-confidence and wise decision making with the energy to move forward.

August / September

MONDAY (AUGUST) SUMMER BANK HOLIDAY (UK-ENG / NIR / WAL)

28

TUESDAY (AUGUST)

29

WEDNESDAY (AUGUST) ○

30

THURSDAY (AUGUST)

31

FRIDAY

1

SATURDAY

2

SUNDAY FATHER'S DAY (AUS / NZ)

3

September 2023

MONDAY LABOR DAY (US) / LABOUR DAY (CAN)

4

TUESDAY

5

WEDNESDAY

6

THURSDAY

7

FRIDAY

8

SATURDAY

9

SUNDAY GRANDPARENTS' DAY (US)

10

SAPPHIRE

Another symbol of purity and wisdom,
sapphire has a calming energy.
Work with it to strengthen belief in
yourself and foster self-esteem.

September 2023

MONDAY PATRIOT DAY (US)   11

TUESDAY   12

WEDNESDAY   13

THURSDAY ●   14

FRIDAY ROSH HASHANAH (BEGINS AT SUNDOWN) /
FIRST DAY OF NATIONAL HISPANIC HERITAGE MONTH

15

SATURDAY

16

SUNDAY

17

I embrace the darkness, for that
is when I see the light.

September 2023

MONDAY 18

TUESDAY 19

WEDNESDAY 20

THURSDAY 21

FRIDAY   22

SATURDAY FALL EQUINOX   23

SUNDAY YOM KIPPUR (BEGINS AT SUNDOWN)   24

Worn, or used in any room of the house,
crystals can help direct energies, offer
protection, decorate, and delight.

October

Necklace for Balancing Chakras

Chakras are an important part of feeling like things are in balance inside and outside of the body. This necklace will be a constant reminder to keep those areas open so that you will thrive with support from the power of the crystals.

What you'll need:

- Carnelian chips for your deepest desires
- Emerald chips for unity in your wants and needs
- Blue lace agate chips for articulation
- A small glass vial with a cork
- Incense
- A small hook eye
- Hot glue gun and glue
- A chain or leather strap for the necklace

1. To cleanse the vial, light some incense, stick it inside the vial, then shake it until the vial becomes opaque.

2. Hold each set of crystal chips to your heart chakra until they feel warm.

3. Bring each cluster near your mouth and speak your intention into them. Then, little by little, add the chips to the vial.

4. Take the hook eye and stick it into the cork, adding some glue to it. Take the hot glue gun and carefully trace the lip of the vial, then insert the cork.

5. As you thread the necklace through the hook and tie it in a knot, recite the following spell aloud and with confidence:

With these crystals plucked from the

Earth and filled with the

power to banish,

I cast these words with most

fervent urge to cleanse, clear,

and halt evil spirits.

OCTOBER 2023

NOTES	SUNDAY	MONDAY	TUESDAY
	1	2	3
		LABOUR DAY (AUS-ACT / NSW / SA)	
	8	9	10
		INDIGENOUS PEOPLES' DAY (US) COLUMBUS DAY (US) THANKSGIVING DAY (CAN)	
	15	16	17
	22	23	24
		LABOUR DAY (NZ)	
	29	30	31
			HALLOWEEN

OCTOBER 2023

WEDNESDAY	THURSDAY	FRIDAY	SATURDAY
4	5 ☽	6	7
			SIMCHAT TORAH (BEGINS AT SUNDOWN)
11	12	13	● 14
18	19	20 ☽	21
25	26	27 ○	28

CARNELIAN

Carnelian is a form of chalcedony whose name derives from the Latin *cornum*, referencing the cornel cherry it resembles. It is an old stone with a rich history. Egyptians sought its protective aura to guide the dead on their journey forward, and the Romans favored this stone for signet rings used to seal official documents—hot wax will not stick to it. It also has a reputation for being one of the luckiest gems available and carries an association with royalty. Carnelian is the warm orange-red color of glowing embers and it will ignite your powers of creativity. It creates a sense of cozy happiness, like gathering around the hearth with friends and family.

 Magical force: Carnelian increases personal power and self confidence, while grounding you in the present moment to be fully in charge. True to its fiery red color, carnelian can also release your passionate side and act as that kick in the pants you need to get things done. Carnelian can also promote fertility for whatever you desire to give birth to.

 Chakra correspondence: *Sacral*—governs creativity and wisdom.

September / October

MONDAY (SEPTEMBER)

25

TUESDAY (SEPTEMBER)

26

WEDNESDAY (SEPTEMBER)

27

THURSDAY (SEPTEMBER)

28

FRIDAY (SEPTEMBER) SUKKOT (BEGINS AT SUNDOWN) ○

29

SATURDAY (SEPTEMBER)

30

SUNDAY

1

October 2023

MONDAY LABOUR DAY (AUS-ACT / NSW / SA)   2

TUESDAY   3

WEDNESDAY   4

THURSDAY   5

FRIDAY 6

SATURDAY SIMCHAT TORAH (BEGINS AT SUNDOWN) 7

SUNDAY 8

OPAL

The opal represents faithfulness and confidence. This stone encourages creativity and emits a protective aura.

October 2023

TUESDAY

10

WEDNESDAY

11

THURSDAY

12

FRIDAY

13

SATURDAY ●

14

SUNDAY

15

*Be attuned to the universal workings
around you and the influence of the
crystal's energy as you work toward
your intentions. Journal about your
experiences, if it helps.*

October 2023

MONDAY   16

TUESDAY   17

WEDNESDAY   18

THURSDAY   19

FRIDAY

20

SATURDAY

21

SUNDAY

22

I feel safe and empowered to speak my truth; I know I can handle whatever may come.

October 2023

MONDAY LABOUR DAY (NZ)

23

TUESDAY

24

WEDNESDAY

25

THURSDAY

26

FRIDAY

27

SATURDAY ○

28

SUNDAY

29

I am an old soul, uplifted by all those who came before me. With these ancient stones, I honor my ancestors.

November

⸻ · Oil for Success · ⸻

However you define it, success is something we all deserve and can achieve with an open mind and focus on manifesting intentions. Bring overall good fortune into your life and help encourage victory in your endeavors. This is best made during the waxing moon.

Gather the following:

- Amber for attracting energy
- Black tourmaline for protection
- A bottle
- Carrier oil
- Star anise for leadership
- Whole cloves to open the way to sweet things
- Dried orange peel to encourage success
- 13 drops of sandalwood oil for abundance

1. Add each ingredient to a bottle, then fill with carrier oil.
2. Hold the bottle to your solar plexus and say the spell on the following page aloud.
3. Leave this oil out in sunlight for 3 days. Then put in a dark place and let sit for at least 3 weeks, shaking every 5 or so days before use.

My success is easily achieved.

It feels amazing to have everything

I have ever wanted.

My gratitude at receiving nonstop

abundance is overflowing.

I am a magnet for prosperity, and my

cup always overflows.

So mote it be!

NOVEMBER 2023

NOTES	SUNDAY	MONDAY	TUESDAY
	5	6	7
			ELECTION DAY (US)
	12	13	14
	FIRST DAY OF DIWALI		
	19	20	21
	26	27	28

NOVEMBER 2023

WEDNESDAY	THURSDAY	FRIDAY	SATURDAY
1 ALL SAINTS' DAY	2	3	4
8	9	10	11 VETERANS DAY (US)
15	16	17	18
22	23 THANKSGIVING DAY (US)	24 NATIVE AMERICAN HERITAGE DAY (US)	25
29	30		

AMBER

Amber is formed of resin from ancient pines that has undergone a complex chemical metamorphosis. It is considered an organic gem, but it is not a crystal or stone. Among the oldest of "crystal" treasures, amber specimens are often more than thirty million years old.

It is a stone of healing as resin's natural purpose is to heal the tree of any wounds sustained. A window into the past, amber often contains fully preserved specimens, both flora and fauna. It is said to be full of life-force energies. Tap into it, if you dare.

Magical force: Wear or carry amber to help when recovering from injury or illness and to instill in you the forces of longevity carried through its millennia of formation. Amber warms to the touch and can be helpful in keeping you grounded and in the moment. Amber breeds patience, especially important when practicing magic and manifesting dreams, and instills happiness.

Chakra correspondences: *Sacral*—ensures the mind and body are functioning as one; *solar plexus*—keeps your immunity at full capacity to fight off potential illness and releases you from fear of judgment, able to live life on your terms.

October / November

MONDAY (OCTOBER)

30

TUESDAY (OCTOBER) HALLOWEEN

31

WEDNESDAY ALL SAINTS' DAY

1

THURSDAY

2

FRIDAY

3

SATURDAY

4

SUNDAY ☽

5

November 2023

MONDAY

6

TUESDAY ELECTION DAY (US)

7

WEDNESDAY

8

THURSDAY

9

FRIDAY 10

SATURDAY VETERANS DAY (US) 11

SUNDAY FIRST DAY OF DIWALI 12

TOPAZ

*Symbolizing love and affection, topaz
promotes honesty, inner wisdom,
and openness.*

November 2023

MONDAY ●   13

TUESDAY   14

WEDNESDAY   15

THURSDAY   16

FRIDAY

17

SATURDAY

18

SUNDAY

19

Believe in your beautiful magic.
It is unique to you but can touch many.

November 2023

MONDAY 20

TUESDAY 21

WEDNESDAY 22

THURSDAY THANKSGIVING DAY (US) 23

FRIDAY NATIVE AMERICAN HERITAGE DAY (US)

24

SATURDAY

25

SUNDAY

26

Use whatever vibrational sound is pleasing to you, and visualize the sound waves carrying the crystal's negative energies away like the breeze.

December

RITUAL

⸂· Circle to See the Future ·⸃

When a glimpse into the future might help you deal with the realities of today, gather your crystal seers to raise your sense of clairvoyance. Building your intuitive skills can help you navigate questions when working on long-term goals and give you a quick gut check on those everyday issues that pop up. Since timelines are subject to change, the key is to focus on the feelings you receive when in this circle.

Gather the following:

- Clear quartz to amplify the other crystals
- Moonstone for seeing through the shadows
- Citrine for seeing through the light
- Blue kyanite to connect to your clair gifts
- Your birthstone to focus on your timeline

Cast a circle with your crystals, form the question in your mind, and say the following spell aloud:

I seek to know beyond the known,

to see what I don't see.

To have the gift of knowing sight

bestowed this day on me.

To guide my actions and my fate

and hint of what's to come,

I wait.

DECEMBER 2023

NOTES	SUNDAY	MONDAY	TUESDAY
	3	4 ☽	5
	INTERNATIONAL DAY OF PERSONS WITH DISABILITIES		
	10	11 ●	12
	HUMAN RIGHTS DAY		
	17	18 ☾	19
	24	25 ○	26
	CHRISTMAS EVE		
	31		BOXING DAY (UK / CAN / AUS / NZ)
	NEW YEAR'S EVE	CHRISTMAS DAY	FIRST DAY OF KWANZAA

DECEMBER 2023

WEDNESDAY	THURSDAY	FRIDAY	SATURDAY
		1 WORLD AIDS DAY	2
6	7 HANUKKAH (BEGINS AT SUNDOWN)	8	9
13	14	15	16
20	21 WINTER SOLSTICE	22	23
27	28	29	30

BLUE KYANITE

Blue kyanite forms from the mineral aluminum silicate. This high-vibrational stone inspires loyalty and thus promotes the ability and desire to heal relationship rifts, whether personal, professional, familial, or other. Blue kyanite also anchors you in the reality of fulfilling your destiny, so quit blaming it on others and get to work! The color of the sky, blue kyanite allows you to soar and gives you the patience needed to get to your desired destination.

Magical force: Use kyanite's vibrational ability in meditation to enhance your clair (psychic) gifts and connect with your spirit wisdom. Its powerful energies are strongly protective—like a shield of armor against life's slings and arrows. Blue kyanite fills you with water's flowing spirit and ability to move around obstacles with ease. Place this crystal under your pillow if you're working to recall and interpret dreams or wish to experience lucid dreams.

Chakra correspondence: Uniquely, all, and especially the *throat* chakra. Kyanite increases the truth and clarity of your communication, especially among opposing viewpoints.

November / December

MONDAY (NOVEMBER) ○

27

TUESDAY (NOVEMBER)

28

WEDNESDAY (NOVEMBER)

29

THURSDAY (NOVEMBER)

30

FRIDAY WORLD AIDS DAY

1

SATURDAY

2

SUNDAY INTERNATIONAL DAY OF PERSONS WITH DISABILITIES

3

December 2023

MONDAY

4

TUESDAY ☽

5

WEDNESDAY

6

THURSDAY HANUKKAH (BEGINS AT SUNDOWN)

7

FRIDAY

8

SATURDAY

9

SUNDAY HUMAN RIGHTS DAY

10

TURQUOISE

Turquoise brings luck and good fortune.
This healing stone heightens your
spiritual attunement and promotes
clear communication, and so can also
promote forgiveness.

December 2023

MONDAY 11

TUESDAY ● 12

WEDNESDAY 13

THURSDAY 14

FRIDAY

15

SATURDAY

16

SUNDAY

17

Crystals that formed slowly over time emit gentler energy vibrations than crystals formed from cosmic force or explosion, whose energies are more intense and immediate.

December 2023

MONDAY

18

TUESDAY

19

WEDNESDAY

20

THURSDAY WINTER SOLSTICE

21

FRIDAY

22

SATURDAY

23

SUNDAY CHRISTMAS EVE

24

Engage in mindful meditation, chakra work, or other self-care rituals that make you feel like the magical being you are. Forgive yourself and others.

December 2023

MONDAY CHRISTMAS DAY
25

TUESDAY BOXING DAY (UK / CAN / AUS / NZ) / FIRST DAY OF KWANZAA ○
26

WEDNESDAY
27

THURSDAY
28

FRIDAY

29

SATURDAY

30

SUNDAY NEW YEAR'S EVE

31

*Though I dream of the future, I embrace
today with joy and gratitude.*

January

RITUAL

⌒ · Selenite for Intuition · ⌒

Selenite has long been associated with consciousness and enlightenment. It is a reliable for unraveling soul knots, those murky and dark inner feelings that, when left unaddressed, can manifest as strife and stifle your intuition.

Your intuition can be your best guide and protector when there's too much information to take in all at once or too little time to synthesize it all. Trust that divine wisdom you've been blessed with. To connect to our intuition and our ability to both hear and be guided by our inner wisdom, selenite can be placed in your space to lend its powerful protective capabilities to you while also serving as a reminder to turn to your own inner third eye.

1. Place one, or a few, selenite stones in your space.

2. Close your eyes and focus on wherever on your person you feel your third eye is located.

3. Picture a light in the darkness radiating from that space within you and covering the entire outside of your body.

4. When you feel ready, say softly or aloud the following spell:

With crystal clarity I accept what the
eyes cannot see but
the heart knows is true.
I trust the light I see within though
darkness may abound.
I conjure this cocoon of light to keep
us safe and sound.

JANUARY 2024

NOTES	SUNDAY	MONDAY	TUESDAY
		1 NEW YEAR'S DAY	2 NEW YEAR HOLIDAY (UK-SCT)
	7	8	9
	14	15 CIVIL RIGHTS DAY (US) MARTIN LUTHER KING JR. DAY (US)	16
	21	22	23
	28	29	30

JANUARY 2024

WEDNESDAY	THURSDAY	FRIDAY	SATURDAY
☽ 3	4	5	6
10	● 11	12	13
◑ 17	18	19	20
24	○ 25	26 AUSTRALIA DAY (AUS)	27 HOLOCAUST REMEMBRANCE DAY
31			

LAPIS LAZULI

Lapis lazuli, a stone of communication, intuition, and personal power, is a metamorphic rock that is composed of numerous minerals, including lazurite, pyrite, and calcite. Its distinct deep-blue color, sometimes with flecks of pyrite, make it a sought-after gemstone, and it's been popular as such for thousands of years. It's worth noting that one of the primary—and oldest—sources for the finest lapis is Afghanistan, where it is often mined and obtained illegally. There are advocacy groups working to have Afghan lapis labeled as a conflict mineral, so be mindful of the source when choosing a lapis stone.

Magical force: Lapis lazuli has a very calming energy, easing all manner of mental and emotional distress and facilitating communication in difficult circumstances. Meditating with lapis can lift your spirit to the heavens and connect you to your spirit guides to receive enlightening messages. It is a stone of friendship and can attract like-minded people to you. Lapis will reinforce your personal power to act for your highest good and draw the respect of others to you.

Chakra correspondences: *Throat*—enhances truth and wisdom in all forms of communication, including with yourself; *third eye*—works as a conduit to one's higher self.

January

MONDAY NEW YEAR'S DAY

1

TUESDAY NEW YEAR HOLIDAY (UK-SCT)

2

WEDNESDAY ☽

3

THURSDAY

4

FRIDAY

5

SATURDAY

6

SUNDAY

7

January 2024

MONDAY

8

TUESDAY

9

WEDNESDAY

10

THURSDAY ●

11

FRIDAY   12

SATURDAY   13

SUNDAY   14

GARNET

Believed to keep its wearer safe while
traveling, garnet has a powerfully
energizing and revitalizing energy;
it also purifies and invites love
and devotion.

January 2024

MONDAY CIVIL RIGHTS DAY (US) / MARTIN LUTHER KING JR. DAY (US)

15

TUESDAY

16

WEDNESDAY

17

THURSDAY

18

FRIDAY

19

SATURDAY

20

SUNDAY

21

I am attuned to the Universal workings around me.

January 2024

MONDAY

22

TUESDAY

23

WEDNESDAY

24

THURSDAY ○

25

FRIDAY AUSTRALIA DAY (AUS)

26

SATURDAY HOLOCAUST REMEMBRANCE DAY

27

SUNDAY

28

*Don't hide your spark. Let it help others
light their path. Acknowledge the spark
in others.*

February

RITUAL

⌁·Tea for Tackling Conflict·⌁

No relationship, romantic or platonic, is without its issues, and it's essential to address them as soon as possible. This tea will help to give you and your loved one the bravery to sit down and sort your issues.

What you'll need:

- Chrysocolla to dispel pain
- Hibiscus for harmony
- Chamomile for stress reduction
- Cornflower for happiness
- Lavender for peace
- Orange peel for truth
- Tea steeper

1. Gather the herbs and orange peel in a steeper, making sure to feel each one before placing them inside. Allow their texture to ground and calm you.

2. Boil some water and pour it in, leaving the herbs to steep for 10 minutes in the boiling water.

3. Before you sip, hold the chrysocolla to your heart chakra and recite the spell on the following page.

4. When you feel ready, place the chrysocolla in your pocket, then invite the other person for some tea and conversation.

When anger does flare, my
patience does wear, and hurtful my
words can be.
With herbs that will soothe,
I pause to infuse my reserves with
kindness and ease.

FEBRUARY 2024

NOTES	SUNDAY	MONDAY	TUESDAY
	4	5	6
			WAITANGI DAY OBSERVED (NZ)
	11	12	13
	18	19	20
		PRESIDENTS' DAY (US)	
	25	26	27

FEBRUARY 2024

WEDNESDAY	THURSDAY	FRIDAY	SATURDAY
	1	2	3
	FIRST DAY OF BLACK HISTORY MONTH	GROUNDHOG DAY (US / CAN)	
7	8	9	10
			CHINESE NEW YEAR
14	15	16	17
VALENTINE'S DAY ASH WEDNESDAY			
21	22	23	24
28	29		

CHRYSOCOLLA

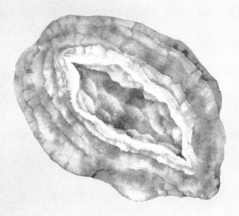

Chrysocolla is a silicate mineral and forms in places where water dissolves copper from the Earth, which contributes to its blue-greenish hue. This gentle, healing stone can bring on peaceful, easy feelings just by looking at it. Chrysocolla's cool color can help you keep your cool and, as such, is a good stone for daily use. As a stone said to encourage staying close to home, it stirs a great acceptance of self.

Magical force: Chrysocolla can help dispel fear, anger, worry, pain, and bad habits—including bad relationships—and empower you to accept the changes needed or just say no to those who don't respect your boundaries, and fill the space by drawing in ease, comfort, wisdom, and forgiveness. It is a stone of new beginnings and the joy they can bring. It can also be used in love spells. Placed in any room of the home, it creates an instant energy oasis.

Chakra correspondences: Said to align all the chakras with the divine, chrysocolla is particularly healing for removing energy blocks of the *third eye*, *throat*, and *heart* chakras.

January / February

MONDAY (JANUARY)

29

TUESDAY (JANUARY)

30

WEDNESDAY (JANUARY)

31

THURSDAY FIRST DAY OF BLACK HISTORY MONTH

1

FRIDAY GROUNDHOG DAY (US / CAN)

2

SATURDAY

3

SUNDAY

4

February 2024

MONDAY

5

TUESDAY WAITANGI DAY OBSERVED (NZ)

6

WEDNESDAY

7

THURSDAY

8

FRIDAY

9

SATURDAY CHINESE NEW YEAR

10

SUNDAY

11

AMETHYST

*At one time only available to royalty,
this stone is thought to build relationships.
Amethyst has a strong healing and calming
vibration, boosts inner strength, and offers
spiritual protection.*

February 2024

MONDAY 12

TUESDAY 13

WEDNESDAY VALENTINE'S DAY / ASH WEDNESDAY 14

THURSDAY 15

FRIDAY

16

SATURDAY

17

SUNDAY

18

*I am a courageous warrior, able
to withstand the battles of life.*

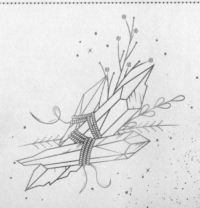

February 2024

MONDAY PRESIDENTS' DAY (US)   19

TUESDAY   20

WEDNESDAY   21

THURSDAY   22

FRIDAY

23

SATURDAY ○

24

SUNDAY

25

Today, I choose joy and confidence.
I am sovereign of my Universe.

March

Relationship Clarity

If things feel a little lackluster in the romance department, or there are rifts in your professional or familial relationships, this crystal combination spell will help dissipate your worries and give you a new perspective.

Materials you'll need:

- Selenite for cleansing negative energy
- Amethyst for clarity
- Sunstone for cleansing the heart
- Malachite for breaking free of negative patterns

1. Take the selenite and circle it around yourself to cleanse your energy.
2. Circle the amethyst around your head to open your third eye for mental clarity.
3. Place sunstone over your heart for an emotional cleansing.
4. Set the crystals around you and place the malachite in front of you.
5. Either lie back or sit up and meditate. Focus on the stones, then hold the malachite in your hand and say:

I vow to be honest and trusting.

To watch for actions and calm

my mind of fear.

I welcome purpose in my life.

Let my passions guide me.

MARCH 2024

NOTES	SUNDAY	MONDAY	TUESDAY
	☾ 3	4	5
	● 10	11	12
	RAMADAN (BEGINS AT SUNDOWN) MOTHERING SUNDAY (UK)	LABOUR DAY (AUS-VIC)	
	☾ 17	18	19
	ST. PATRICK'S DAY		SPRING EQUINOX
	24 PALM SUNDAY	○ 25	26
	31 EASTER		

MARCH 2024

WEDNESDAY	THURSDAY	FRIDAY	SATURDAY
		1 FIRST DAY OF WOMEN'S HISTORY MONTH	2
6	7	8	9
13	14	15	16
20 NOWRUZ	21	22	23 PURIM (BEGINS AT SUNDOWN)
27	28	29 GOOD FRIDAY	30

SUNSTONE

Sunstone, also known as heliolite, is a feldspar, usually translucent, that exhibits lovely bright flashes of light like little bursts of sunshine. Sunstone has been known for only a few hundred years; the most famous, and best, deposits are in Oregon, discovered by Indigenous Peoples living in that region who treasured its beauty as a gift from Mother Earth. This fiery stone breeds passion and life and is a happy-go-lucky crystal. Wear sunstone to increase your vitality and let your inner being shine.

 Magical force: Sunstone will ignite your passion and power. Its warming vibrations encourage you to open yourself to opportunities and revel in the moment. It is a source of strength and light in times of darkness and can boost your intuition in meditation. Sunstone encourages optimism and enthusiasm and releases you from fear of others' judgment. It envelops you in a reflective barrier, off of which all negative energy ricochets.

 Chakra correspondence: All, especially the *root* chakra, like the Sun, the source of all energy for the body and seat of personal power.

February / March

MONDAY (FEBRUARY)

26

TUESDAY (FEBRUARY)

27

WEDNESDAY (FEBRUARY)

28

THURSDAY (FEBRUARY)

29

FRIDAY FIRST DAY OF WOMEN'S HISTORY MONTH

1

SATURDAY

2

SUNDAY ☽

3

March 2024

MONDAY

4

TUESDAY

5

WEDNESDAY

6

THURSDAY

7

FRIDAY

8

SATURDAY

9

SUNDAY RAMADAN (BEGINS AT SUNDOWN) / MOTHERING SUNDAY (UK) ●

10

AQUAMARINE

Aquamarine's energies help release anger, relieve stress, and raise the tides of courage to flow with whatever life throws at you.

March 2024

MONDAY LABOUR DAY (AUS-VIC)

11

TUESDAY

12

WEDNESDAY

13

THURSDAY

14

FRIDAY

15

SATURDAY

16

SUNDAY ST. PATRICK'S DAY

17

*I call sweet sleep to lie with me, to sing
a lullaby—to wake renewed, with energy
to set the world on fire.*

March 2024

MONDAY 18

TUESDAY SPRING EQUINOX 19

WEDNESDAY NOWRUZ 20

THURSDAY 21

FRIDAY

22

SATURDAY PURIM (BEGINS AT SUNDOWN)

23

SUNDAY PALM SUNDAY

24

Incorporate gratitude into your journaling for all the positive influences you have access to in your life.

March 2024

MONDAY ○   25

TUESDAY   26

WEDNESDAY   27

THURSDAY   28

FRIDAY GOOD FRIDAY

29

SATURDAY

30

SUNDAY EASTER

31

Having an altar as a dedicated magical space for you to work is optional, but a dedicated crystal altar can be a fun space to create and use in your magical practice to inspire your work.

April

Oil for Grounding

This oil recipe helps realign a possibly blocked root chakra and helps reconnect your mind and body to renew a sense of stability and grounding within yourself. The smell of this oil is extremely important, since it's recommended that you wear it as a perfume. As you add each item to the jar, recite the spell on the following page.

Gather the following:

- Hematite
- Smoky quartz
- Black tourmaline
- 1 small piece of green jade
- A cleansed jar

- Skin-safe carrier oil
- Yarrow oil
- Lavender oil
- Chamomile oil
- Jasmine oil

1. Add all of the elements to a cleansed jar.
2. Fill with preferred skin-safe carrier oil almost to the top, close the lid, and shake gently to combine.
3. Dab the oil on the front and back of your root chakra.

Prepare the ground have I to cradle,

raise, and nurture well.

For when I hear the Earth's winsome

tune my heart embraces the

hope to swell.

APRIL 2024

NOTES	SUNDAY	MONDAY	TUESDAY
		☽ 1	2
		APRIL FOOLS' DAY	
	7	● 8	9
			EID AL-FITR (BEGINS AT SUNDOWN)
	14	☽ 15	16
	21	22	○ 23
		PASSOVER (BEGINS AT SUNDOWN) EARTH DAY	
	28	29	30

APRIL 2024

WEDNESDAY	THURSDAY	FRIDAY	SATURDAY
3	4	5	6
10	11	12	13
17	18	19	20
24 ADMINISTRATIVE PROFESSIONALS' DAY (US)	25 ANZAC DAY (AUS / NZ)	26	27

GREEN JADE

Jade is a type of metamorphic rock that comes in a rainbow of colors—green is the most highly valued. In addition to jewelry made from jade, its durability also made it significant for fashioning into weapons and exquisitely melodic musical instruments. Jade can variously symbolize heaven, nobility, longevity, virtue, wealth, and protection and is called the stone of the heart. Legend tells us that jade that becomes chipped has just taken the brunt of a blow meant for you.

 Magical force: The color green typically symbolizes lush growth and vitality, and green jade brings all that in all areas of life. It is thought to protect and speak wisely to the loving heart, with lessons that sharing our abundance is at the root of true happiness. Gentle jade is a calm, serene stone, so keep some nearby if your nerves of confidence are a-jangle. It is as useful in meditation work as it is in dreamwork. Count yourself lucky to have jade in your possession: its magic will amplify yours.

Chakra correspondence: *Heart*—maintains healing and balance.

April

MONDAY APRIL FOOLS' DAY

1

TUESDAY

2

WEDNESDAY

3

THURSDAY

4

FRIDAY

5

SATURDAY

6

SUNDAY

7

April 2024

MONDAY ●   **8**

TUESDAY EID AL-FITR (BEGINS AT SUNDOWN)   **9**

WEDNESDAY   **10**

THURSDAY   **11**

FRIDAY

12

SATURDAY

13

SUNDAY

14

DIAMOND

A symbol of everlasting love, the diamond is also believed to instill courage. However, a diamond worn for effect or prestige will bring the opposite in love.

April 2024

15

16

17

18

FRIDAY

19

SATURDAY

20

SUNDAY

21

It is clear: I am beautiful. I am wise.
I am love. I am light. I am enough.

April 2024

MONDAY PASSOVER (BEGINS AT SUNDOWN) / EARTH DAY

22

TUESDAY ○

23

WEDNESDAY ADMINISTRATIVE PROFESSIONALS' DAY (US)

24

THURSDAY ANZAC DAY (AUS / NZ)

25

FRIDAY

26

SATURDAY

27

SUNDAY

28

The sky has no limit and neither do my talents.

May

RITUAL

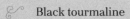

ᴄ· Black Tourmaline Protection ·ↄ

Whether an energetic sabotage from a jealous coworker or pressure-packed meetings, vexing neighbors, self-doubt, or general unease, black tourmaline can block, purify, and reflect negative energies, allowing you to breathe easier and go about your business confident of the outcomes.

Gather the following:

- Black tourmaline
- Salt

- Small, black box—it can be wood, cardboard, whatever you have handy

1. Pour the salt in the box until the bottom is covered, then place the black tourmaline stone in it. As you do, recite the spell on the following page.

2. At least once a week, open the box gently, lower your face to it and speak all your complaints, worries, and problems inside it, then speak the spell.

3. After you're done, close the box quickly. The salt, stone, and color of the box will absorb your troubles. A few words to direct your intentions can amplify its properties.

Once a month, change out the salt in the box and recharge the black tourmaline for one week in the sunshine.

Under your spell I remain undeterred,

for cloaked in your charms

I am safe and assured.

MAY 2024

NOTES	SUNDAY	MONDAY	TUESDAY
	5	6	7
	CINCO DE MAYO ORTHODOX EASTER	LABOUR DAY (AUS–QLD) EARLY MAY BANK HOLIDAY (UK)	
	12	13	14
	MOTHER'S DAY (US / CAN)		
	19	20	21
		VICTORIA DAY (CAN)	
	26	27	28
		SPRING BANK HOLIDAY (UK) MEMORIAL DAY (US)	

MAY 2024

WEDNESDAY	THURSDAY	FRIDAY	SATURDAY
☽ 1 FIRST DAY OF ASIAN AMERICAN AND PACIFIC ISLANDER HERITAGE MONTH	2	3	4 YOM HASHOAH (BEGINS AT SUNDOWN)
8	9	10	11
☽ 15	16	17	18
22 ○	23	24	25
29 ☽	30	31	

BLACK TOURMALINE

Black tourmaline is of the boron silicate family. Black (also called schorl) is the most commonly occurring color of tourmaline, though it is widely available in a rainbow of colors. Historically, those practicing the magical arts used black tourmaline to keep evil away. It is one of the most powerfully protecting stones, forming a shield of sorts, blocking negative and harmful energies, and reflecting them back to their source—where they belong! Tourmaline can be a distinct asset in times of struggle, not only suggesting solutions but also pinpointing the real cause of the distress.

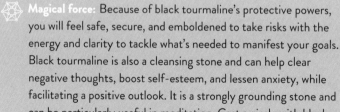

Magical force: Because of black tourmaline's protective powers, you will feel safe, secure, and emboldened to take risks with the energy and clarity to tackle what's needed to manifest your goals. Black tourmaline is also a cleansing stone and can help clear negative thoughts, boost self-esteem, and lessen anxiety, while facilitating a positive outlook. It is a strongly grounding stone and can be particularly useful in meditation. Cast a circle with black tourmaline for ritual work.

Chakra correspondence: *Root*—establishes feelings of safety and security due to its grounding properties.

April / May

MONDAY (APRIL)   29

TUESDAY (APRIL)   30

WEDNESDAY   FIRST DAY OF ASIAN AMERICAN AND
            PACIFIC ISLANDER HERITAGE MONTH   1

THURSDAY   2

FRIDAY   3

SATURDAY   YOM HASHOAH (BEGINS AT SUNDOWN)   4

SUNDAY   CINCO DE MAYO / ORTHODOX EASTER   5

May 2024

MONDAY LABOUR DAY (AUS-QLD) / EARLY MAY BANK HOLIDAY (UK)

6

TUESDAY

7

WEDNESDAY

8

THURSDAY

9

FRIDAY   10

SATURDAY   11

SUNDAY MOTHER'S DAY (US / CAN)   12

EMERALD

A sign of wisdom, growth, and patience,
the emerald helps release negative
energy and opens your heart to love
and the power of inner strength.

May 2024

MONDAY

13

TUESDAY

14

WEDNESDAY

15

THURSDAY

16

FRIDAY

17

SATURDAY

18

SUNDAY

19

*Use what spells speak to you, modify
to suit your needs, or create your own
glittering spells. You have the magic
within to accomplish anything your
heart desires, and it's time to let it shine!*

May 2024

TUESDAY

21

WEDNESDAY

22

THURSDAY ○

23

FRIDAY

24

SATURDAY

25

SUNDAY

26

Incorporating your birthstone into your crystal magic work increases those good vibrational energies even more. Wearing your birthstone is said to bring good luck and good health.

June

RITUAL

⌁ Summoning Healing Spirits ⌁

All matters of ailing can be tended to by these healing spirits. The best outcomes for rituals like this happen when working on your own behalf, but when only healing is intended, you may also perform this on behalf of others.

On your altar, gather:

- Celestite to open heavenly communication
- Almonds, as an offering to invoke the healing powers of the spirits
- Small glass of pure water
- A blue (calming energy) or red (warming energy) candle for healing

1. Place the almonds, water, and celestite on your altar as an offering.
2. Light the candle; its energy will help release your prayer into the world.
3. Take a moment in silent meditation to call forth the spirits whose healing powers you seek. Visualize them with you. Acknowledge their presence.
4. Recite the following spell three times to seal the healing energy.

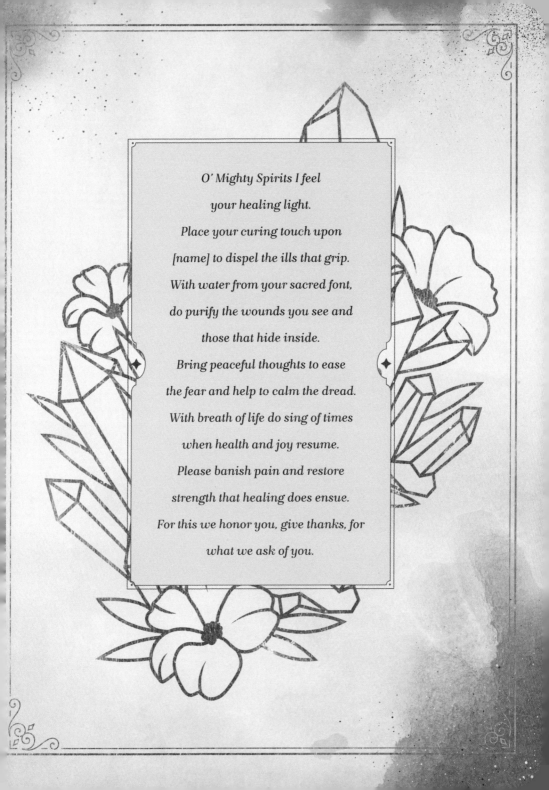

O' Mighty Spirits I feel

your healing light.

Place your curing touch upon

[name] to dispel the ills that grip.

With water from your sacred font,

do purify the wounds you see and

those that hide inside.

Bring peaceful thoughts to ease

the fear and help to calm the dread.

With breath of life do sing of times

when health and joy resume.

Please banish pain and restore

strength that healing does ensue.

For this we honor you, give thanks, for

what we ask of you.

JUNE 2024

NOTES	SUNDAY	MONDAY	TUESDAY
	2	3	4
	9	10	11
	16	17	18
	FATHER'S DAY (US / CAN / UK) 23	24	25
	30		

JUNE 2024

WEDNESDAY	THURSDAY	FRIDAY	SATURDAY
			1
			FIRST DAY OF PRIDE MONTH
5 ●	6	7	8
12	13 ◑	14	15
		FLAG DAY (US)	
19	20 ○	21	22
JUNETEENTH (US)	**SUMMER SOLSTICE**		
26	27 ◐	28	29

CELESTITE

From the Latin word *caelestis*, meaning "celestial," celestite is a conduit of heavenly communication and a vibration connection to our intuitive senses. Celestite's makeup is of strontium sulfate and it is the primary natural source of strontium, an element used to create red (not blue, that's copper) fireworks. Its soothing energies are a balm for our worries and can aid in healing sadness and grief. Its dreamy qualities are especially conducive to peaceful sleep.

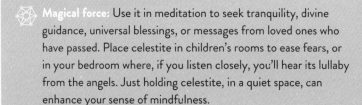

Magical force: Use it in meditation to seek tranquility, divine guidance, universal blessings, or messages from loved ones who have passed. Place celestite in children's rooms to ease fears, or in your bedroom where, if you listen closely, you'll hear its lullaby from the angels. Just holding celestite, in a quiet space, can enhance your sense of mindfulness.

Chakra correspondences: *Throat*—boosts our ability to express what we feel. *Third eye*—allows higher energies to flow in, promoting ease and giving us the wisdom to accept what we cannot change or control and the vision to change what we can. *Crown*—helps access the realm beyond.

MONDAY (MAY) SPRING BANK HOLIDAY (UK) / MEMORIAL DAY (US)

27

TUESDAY (MAY)

28

WEDNESDAY (MAY)

29

THURSDAY (MAY) ☽

30

FRIDAY (MAY)

31

SATURDAY FIRST DAY OF PRIDE MONTH

1

SUNDAY

2

June 2024

MONDAY

3

TUESDAY

4

WEDNESDAY

5

THURSDAY ●

6

FRIDAY

7

SATURDAY

8

SUNDAY

9

PEARL

The pearl is a traditional symbol of purity and inner wisdom. Although not a true crystal, pearls can be worn to magnify loyalty, truth, and sincerity.

June 2024

MONDAY

10

TUESDAY

11

WEDNESDAY

12

THURSDAY

13

FRIDAY FLAG DAY (US)

14

SATURDAY

15

SUNDAY FATHER'S DAY (US / CAN / UK)

16

I am a multihued being, capable of accomplishing anything I put my mind to.

June 2024

MONDAY
17

TUESDAY
18

WEDNESDAY JUNETEENTH (US)
19

THURSDAY SUMMER SOLSTICE
20

FRIDAY ○

21

SATURDAY

22

SUNDAY

23

Notice the sense of peace and fulfilment
you get when you align desires, thoughts,
and actions—intentionally.

June 2024

24

25

26

27

FRIDAY 28

SATURDAY 29

SUNDAY 30

*If you have unanswered questions, take
a moment to close your eyes, center
yourself, and check in with your heart
intuition for guidance.*

July

RITUAL

Gratitude of Love

Appreciating your loved ones for who they are and what they bring to your life is a practice we must not forget to do. Giving thanks to Mother Moon acknowledges how she's helped you along and is a way to feed more love into your life.

What you'll need:

- Green aventurine
- A photo of you and your loved one
- A red candle for deep love
- Sugar to taste and to extract positive energies

1. Perform this ritual right before a Full Moon.
2. Have your loved one touch the green aventurine crystal and obtain a photo of them. This will impart some of their energy.
3. Light the candle and place the green aventurine on top of the picture.
4. Place your fingers on the crystals and focus on what makes your relationship special, what you have now that you've never had before, and how lucky you are to have found each other. Taste the sugar to help extract those positive energies.
5. Then, say the following spell:

Mother Moon, thank you for

the love who's mine.

Who enriches my life and

who's so divine.

May our love last and accrue.

May it stay pure and always be true.

JULY 2024

NOTES	SUNDAY	MONDAY	TUESDAY
		1	2
		CANADA DAY (CAN)	
	7	8	9
	14	15	16
	○ 21	22	23
	28	29	30

JULY 2024

WEDNESDAY	THURSDAY	FRIDAY	SATURDAY
3	4	5	6
	INDEPENDENCE DAY (US)		
10	11	12	13
17	18	19	20
24	25	26	27
31			

GREEN AVENTURINE

Although aventurine comes in many colors, if green aventurine is in your crystal collection, count yourself lucky, as this stone is one of the luckiest of all. This lovely crystal is a type of quartz that connects you to the soothing energy of Nature. Called the "gambler's stone," this ancient crystal is said to bring luck in all manner and form and can even make sure you're in the right place at the right time to take advantage of said luck! It glows with optimism and good fortune and keeps you perpetually on the sunny side of the street. Pick up green aventurine whenever a little lucky magic wouldn't hurt your chances of success, or when you need to ditch a bad habit that may be standing between you and your dreams.

Magical force: Green aventurine is particularly useful in money spells, or carried as a lucky charm at the casino! It can also strengthen your courage to seize the lucky moments when they come and boost overall feelings of happiness and satisfaction.

Chakra correspondence: *Heart*—boosts late-in-life romance and calms family strife. And, with an open heart, you'll hear Lady Luck most clearly when she calls your name.

July

MONDAY CANADA DAY (CAN)

1

TUESDAY

2

WEDNESDAY

3

THURSDAY INDEPENDENCE DAY (US)

4

FRIDAY ●

5

SATURDAY

6

SUNDAY

7

July 2024

MONDAY

8

TUESDAY

9

WEDNESDAY

10

THURSDAY

11

FRIDAY

12

SATURDAY

13

SUNDAY

14

BLOODSTONE

*A magical stone filled with ancient
lore, bloodstone is especially powerful
for weather magic, matters of family
love, money, calming fears, and
instilling courage—no matter the
battle being fought.*

July 2024

MONDAY 15

TUESDAY 16

WEDNESDAY 17

THURSDAY 18

FRIDAY   19

SATURDAY   20

SUNDAY ⟳   21

Breathe in creativity; breathe out
boredom. Breathe in love; breathe
out negativity.

July 2024

FRIDAY 26

SATURDAY  27

SUNDAY 28

I emerge from the fire stronger than before. I will survive and shine brighter than ever.

August

RITUAL

⌁·Banish Negative Energy·⌁

Sometimes, negativity is two-fold, and can be produced by your own thoughts as well as outside influences. Whether the energy is attacking from outside or within, to protect yourself, you'll need:

- Labradorite for shielding from ill-will
- Amethyst to amplify energy
- A small jar
- Rosemary for fighting evil spirits
- Honeysuckle for peace
- A black candle to seal the jar
- Black salt as a barrier

1. Place the herbs in the jar one at a time, focusing on their intention.
2. Then, hold the crystals in your hand, enclose them in your fist, close your eyes, and imagine your strong will flowing from your hands into the crystals to charge them. Infuse them with your energy.
3. Place them in the jar.
4. Place the black candle on top, light it, and let it coat the jar.
5. Then, say the spell on the following page quietly or aloud.
6. Take the jar and your black salt outside to your garden or backyard. Bury the jar so it leaves no bump.
7. Finally, sprinkle the black salt around your property, imagining there's a shield going up.

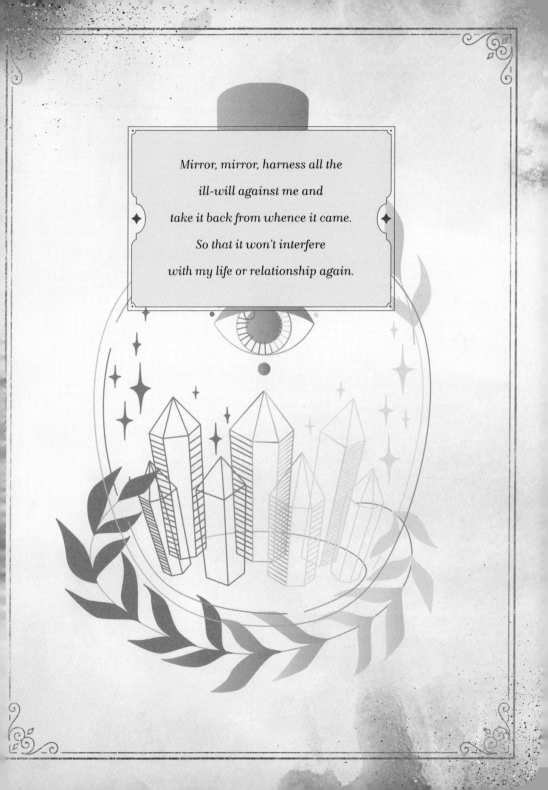

Mirror, mirror, harness all the

ill-will against me and

take it back from whence it came.

So that it won't interfere

with my life or relationship again.

AUGUST 2024

NOTES	SUNDAY	MONDAY	TUESDAY
	● 4	5	6
		SUMMER BANK HOLIDAY (UK-SCT)	
	11	◗ 12	13
	18	○ 19	20
	25	◖ 26	27
		SUMMER BANK HOLIDAY (UK-ENG / NIR / WAL)	

AUGUST 2024

WEDNESDAY	THURSDAY	FRIDAY	SATURDAY
	1	2	3
7	8	9	10
14	15	16	17
21	22	23	24
28	29	30	31

LABRADORITE

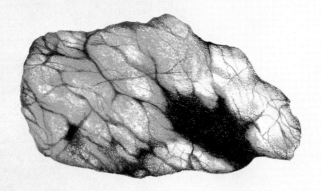

Labradorite is a variety of feldspar named for its place of discovery in Labrador, Canada. This mystical, magical, multihued stone is as flashy as a peacock in full display (the colorful effect is called labradorescence) and believed, by the Inuit, to have fallen to Earth from the aurora borealis. As such, it brings powers to increase clairvoyance, and its energies will surround you in a magical cloak of protection, blocking negative energy. But labradorite will also keep you grounded, so as not to lose your head in the clouds. This beauty is the stone of new beginnings and limitless potential. Labradorite discourages antisocial behavior and encourages courtesy and friendliness.

Magical force: Gazing into this mystical stone is like peeking through the curtain to the other side. Try scrying or meditating with labradorite. It is a marker of change and a reminder of strength to embrace it. Place a piece under your pillow to tap into the unconscious realm of your dreams.

Chakra correspondence: All, but especially the *third eye*, labradorite aligns mental, physical, and spiritual power for the highest vibrational energies.

MONDAY (JULY)

29

TUESDAY (JULY)

30

WEDNESDAY (JULY)

31

THURSDAY

1

FRIDAY

2

SATURDAY

3

SUNDAY ●

4

August 2024

MONDAY SUMMER BANK HOLIDAY (UK-SCT)

5

TUESDAY

6

WEDNESDAY

7

THURSDAY

8

FRIDAY

9

SATURDAY

10

SUNDAY

11

FAIRY STONE

*Fairy stones can connect your mind
and heart to the spirit realm. They also
bring good luck and offer protection
from illness and negative energies—and
evil spirits—as well as call wealth and
abundance to you.*

August 2024

MONDAY 12

TUESDAY 13

WEDNESDAY 14

THURSDAY 15

FRIDAY

16

SATURDAY

17

SUNDAY

18

I am receptive to the messages of the
Universe that guide me to my highest self.

August 2024

19

20

21

22

FRIDAY

23

SATURDAY

24

SUNDAY

25

*I step bravely into discomfort, for that
is where I grow.*

September

RITUAL

~·Potpourri for Happiness·~

A potpourri bundle of fresh herbs and crystals will give off the energy of your intention and provide you with an uplifting talisman made from the heart. This bundle works similar to a charm bag, but is more discreet and on a larger scale.

What you'll need:

- Garnet for happiness
- Tiger's eye for health
- Lemurian seed crystal
- Rose quartz for love
- Dill for manifestation
- Lemon balm for wellness
- Lavender for peace
- A medium-sized drawstring bag

1. Take each herb and crystal out of its container and feel them with your hands.

2. Place the herbs and crystals strategically in the bag as you recite the spell on the following page.

3. Hold the bag to your heart and envision a moment that you felt joyful, reveling in the emotion.

I need the peace of living life that

doesn't dwell in fears.

I ask to be uplifted and to feel

my burdens ease,

I'm ready to reclaim my joy and

leave behind dis-ease.

SEPTEMBER 2024

NOTES	SUNDAY	MONDAY	TUESDAY
	1	2 ●	3
	FATHER'S DAY (AUS / NZ)	LABOR DAY (US) LABOUR DAY (CAN)	
	8	9	10
	GRANDPARENTS' DAY (US)		
	15	16	17 ○
	FIRST DAY OF NATIONAL HISPANIC HERITAGE MONTH		
	22	23	24 ◗
	FALL EQUINOX		
	29	30	

SEPTEMBER 2024

WEDNESDAY	THURSDAY	FRIDAY	SATURDAY
4	5	6	7
11 PATRIOT DAY (US)	12	13	14
18	19	20	21
25	26	27	28

LEMURIAN SEED

The origins of the Lemurian seed crystal are steeped in mystic lore, in the peaceful and mythical kingdom of Lemuria, located in the South Pacific region. Legend tells us that the Lemurians foresaw a disastrous event and, in order to preserve their knowledge, wisdom, and traditions, embedded, or coded, them all into these crystals.

These wand-like crystals come in a variety of colors and can be identified by their tactile parallel striations, or markings, noted as resembling bar codes. Some say their source is a single mine in Brazil; others say these crystals can be found the world over. Whatever your beliefs, the energy these crystals emit is unmistakable and magical in its own right.

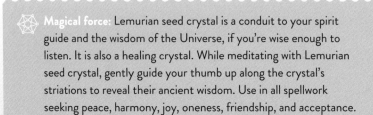

Magical force: Lemurian seed crystal is a conduit to your spirit guide and the wisdom of the Universe, if you're wise enough to listen. It is also a healing crystal. While meditating with Lemurian seed crystal, gently guide your thumb up along the crystal's striations to reveal their ancient wisdom. Use in all spellwork seeking peace, harmony, joy, oneness, friendship, and acceptance.

Chakra correspondence: All, and particularly the *third eye*. At its best, Lemurian seed crystal harmonizes and heals.

August / September

MONDAY (AUGUST) SUMMER BANK HOLIDAY (UK-ENG / NIR / WAL) 26

TUESDAY (AUGUST) 27

WEDNESDAY (AUGUST) 28

THURSDAY (AUGUST) 29

FRIDAY (AUGUST) 30

SATURDAY (AUGUST) 31

SUNDAY FATHER'S DAY (AUS / NZ) 1

September 2024

MONDAY LABOR DAY (US) / LABOUR DAY (CAN) ● 2

TUESDAY 3

WEDNESDAY 4

THURSDAY 5

FRIDAY

6

SATURDAY

7

SUNDAY GRANDPARENTS' DAY (US)

8

AMAZONITE

Amazonite is a stone of protection, blocking and cleansing away general aura pollution. And, like the flowing waters this stone is named for, amazonite teaches you to go with the flow.

September 2024

MONDAY   9

TUESDAY   10

WEDNESDAY PATRIOT DAY (US)   11

THURSDAY   12

FRIDAY

13

SATURDAY

14

SUNDAY FIRST DAY OF NATIONAL HISPANIC HERITAGE MONTH

15

*Breathe in the joyful, life-giving qualities
of the Sun; breathe out fear.*

September 2024

MONDAY

16

TUESDAY ○

17

WEDNESDAY

18

THURSDAY

19

FRIDAY

20

SATURDAY

21

SUNDAY FALL EQUINOX

22

*Strength and abundance radiate from
me with ease.*

September 2024

MONDAY

23

TUESDAY

24

WEDNESDAY

25

THURSDAY

26

FRIDAY

27

SATURDAY

28

SUNDAY

29

I am a sum of all my emotions,
without judgment.

October

Fortunate Futures

It may not be possible for the future to be revealed, but putting out your energies and praying for specific desires can help the Universe understand what you need. For the best outcomes, bring energies of openness and creativity to the ritual, allowing yourself to be led by an optimistic action of change, rather than through resentment or pessimism.

Gather the following:

- Prehnite
- Pen and paper
- A candle
- Cauldron or a heat-safe surface

1. On your paper, write down your desired outcome.
2. Light the candle.
3. Light the paper in your cauldron and watch the flames turn your intentions into fertile ash.
4. Hold prehnite and envision yourself capable of creating change and calling on your own powers to shift your reality.
5. When ready, recite the spell on the following page.
6. Extinguish the candle and watch the rising smoke take your prayer into the cosmos, where it will be received and answered.

From the ground I thee pluck

this little bit of turnaround luck.

Forgotten and discarded

into something still regarded,

this trash into treasure

in my fortune I will find pleasure.

OCTOBER 2024

NOTES	SUNDAY	MONDAY	TUESDAY
....			1
....			
....			
....			
....	6	7	8
....			
....			
....		LABOUR DAY (AUS-ACT / NSW / SA)	
....	13	14	15
....		INDIGENOUS PEOPLES' DAY (US)	
....		COLUMBUS DAY (US)	
....		THANKSGIVING DAY (CAN)	
....	20	21	22
....			
....			
....	27	28	29
....			
....			
....		LABOUR DAY (NZ)	

OCTOBER 2024

WEDNESDAY	THURSDAY	FRIDAY	SATURDAY
● 2 ROSH HASHANAH (BEGINS AT SUNDOWN)	3	4	5
9	◐ 10	11 YOM KIPPUR (BEGINS AT SUNDOWN)	12
16 ○	17	18	19
SUKKOT (BEGINS AT SUNDOWN)			
23 ◑	24 SIMCHAT TORAH (BEGINS AT SUNDOWN)	25	26
30	31 FIRST DAY OF DIWALI HALLOWEEN		

PREHNITE

Prehnite is a silicate mineral, typically beautifully green in color, discovered in South Africa in the eighteenth century. Called the stone of prophecy, it has a lovely magical energy and can induce that sense of déjà vu. Prehnite is particularly useful when manifesting intentions that come from the heart. Prehnite's energies will help align yours with Nature, as well as opening your heart to unconditional love and your mind to new ideas.

 Magical force: Prehnite provides special energy to attract angels and fairies (and offers an orb of protective energy from random encounters with evil fairies). It is said to enhance your prophetic senses, such as clairvoyance, clairaudience, and claircognizance, so add it to your scrying crystals or tarot sessions for clearer communications with spirit guides (pay special attention to your dreams afterward). Used in meditation, prehnite keeps you grounded in the present and abundantly happy. Prehnite is particularly powerful in crystal grids for abundance.

 Chakra correspondence: *Heart*—heals wounds of past loves lost, opens you to receive new love, eases anxiety.

September / October

MONDAY (SEPTEMBER)

30

TUESDAY

1

WEDNESDAY ROSH HASHANAH (BEGINS AT SUNDOWN) ●

2

THURSDAY

3

FRIDAY

4

SATURDAY

5

SUNDAY

6

October 2024

MONDAY <small>LABOUR DAY (AUS-ACT / NSW / SA)</small>

7

TUESDAY

8

WEDNESDAY

9

THURSDAY ◖

10

FRIDAY YOM KIPPUR (BEGINS AT SUNDOWN)   11

SATURDAY   12

SUNDAY   13

CLEAR QUARTZ

Clear quartz is among the most powerful crystals when working to manifest intentions. It is believed to be a universal soother and healer and, among other things, encourages positive thoughts, enhances energy, and brings vision into focus.

October 2024

MONDAY INDIGENOUS PEOPLES' DAY (US) / COLUMBUS DAY (US) / THANKSGIVING DAY (CAN)

14

TUESDAY

15

WEDNESDAY SUKKOT (BEGINS AT SUNDOWN)

16

THURSDAY ○

17

FRIDAY   18 .

SATURDAY   19

SUNDAY   20

Honor the Earth for her crystal gifts and
thank your crystals for their illuminating
presence in your life.

October 2024

MONDAY

21

TUESDAY

22

WEDNESDAY

23

THURSDAY SIMCHAT TORAH (BEGINS AT SUNDOWN)

24

FRIDAY

25

SATURDAY

26

SUNDAY

27

Breathe in the messages of the Universe;
breathe out gratitude.

November

⟶ Tarot for Love ⟵

In this ritual, you will use tarot's powerful messages for your specific purpose. To perform this spell, you must have a loving relationship with yourself and be able to allow your preconceived notions of love and romance to be shaken.

You'll need:

- Moonstone for your inner goddess
- Red jasper for goddess energy
- Rose quartz for love
- Two pink candles
- Jasmine oil
- The Lovers card
- The Tower card

To enact the spell:

1. Anoint the candles with jasmine oil. Set them on either end of your altar and light them.

2. Take the picture of you and The Lovers card and place them in front of each of the candles.

3. Place The Tower card in between the two candles.

4. Place the moonstone and red jasper underneath The Tower.

5. Touch the moonstone and red jasper, then thank the Moon for blessing the ritual.

6. Place the quartz near your picture, then move them over to The Lovers card. Imagine pulling the essence of your object with your hands and then placing it onto The Lovers.

7. Recite the following spell three times:

Mother Moon, I speak my

intentions to you.

Bless me with a lasting love

so I may feel as though

you've chosen them from above.

NOVEMBER 2024

NOTES	SUNDAY	MONDAY	TUESDAY
	3	4	5
			ELECTION DAY (US)
	10	11	12
		VETERANS DAY (US)	
	17	18	19
	24	25	26

NOVEMBER 2024

WEDNESDAY	THURSDAY	FRIDAY	SATURDAY
		● 1 ALL SAINTS' DAY	2
6	7	8 ◗	9
13	14 ○ 15		16
20	21 ◗ 22		23
27	28 THANKSGIVING DAY (US)	29 NATIVE AMERICAN HERITAGE DAY (US)	30

MOONSTONE

Mysterious, glowing moonstone is a variety of the feldspar mineral group.
It is found in a number of colors, including gray, peach, rainbow, and white.
Moonstone, once believed to have originated from moonbeams themselves, is a
stone of new beginnings, fertility, destiny, and wishes. It is also one of reflection,
helping you look within and find forgiveness. Enchantingly beautiful, moonstone
traditionally helps us connect to the natural ebb and flow of the Moon's energy. If
you're dealing with high emotions, or are in need of restoring calm and balance,
this could be the stone for you.

Magical force: Place moonstone under your pillow to inspire
prophetic dreams. Incorporate moonstone into any Moon magic
work, and to summon your inner goddess. Carry moonstone for
good luck. Legend says if you hold a moonstone in your mouth on
the night of the Full Moon, your future will be revealed.

Chakra correspondences: *Third eye*—restores a balance of
emotions and instills patience; *crown*—increases intuitive abilities,
expands your vision, and allows you to feel at peace with your
place in the Universe.

October/November

MONDAY (OCTOBER) LABOUR DAY (NZ)

28

TUESDAY (OCTOBER)

29

WEDNESDAY (OCTOBER)

30

THURSDAY (OCTOBER) HALLOWEEN / FIRST DAY OF DIWALI

31

FRIDAY ALL SAINTS' DAY

1

SATURDAY

2

SUNDAY

3

November 2024

MONDAY

4

TUESDAY ELECTION DAY (US)

5

WEDNESDAY

6

THURSDAY

7

FRIDAY

8

SATURDAY

9

SUNDAY

10

CORDIERITE (Iolite)

Use this dusk-colored stone at twilight when casting spells for banishing bad habits, managing money for abundance, restoring motivation, and sorting out priorities to double its effect.

November 2024

TUESDAY 12

WEDNESDAY 13

THURSDAY 14

FRIDAY ○

15

SATURDAY

16

SUNDAY

17

*I choose to see beyond that which is
physical; I believe in the power of magic.*

November 2024

MONDAY

18

TUESDAY

19

WEDNESDAY

20

THURSDAY

21

FRIDAY 22

SATURDAY 23

SUNDAY 24

I feel safe and empowered to speak my truth; I know I can handle whatever may come.

December

⌁·Amulet for Friends·⌁

Invisible influences exist everywhere, and your friends won't always have you to look out for them. Give them this amulet to promote positivity when you can't be there to uplift them.

You will need these materials:

- Hematite chip for strength
- Yellow quartz for happiness
- A small glass vial with a cork
- Dried daisy for friendship
- Cinnamon for protection
- A small hook and eye
- Hot glue gun and glue
- Black chain or leather strap

1. Drop the herbs into the vial one at a time, filling it about a fourth of the way.

2. Place the crystals inside the vial as you recite the spell on the following page.

3. Take the hook eye and stick it into the cork, adding some glue to it.

4. Carefully add a line of glue along the lip of the vial and seal it with the cork.

5. Thread your strap of choice through the hook.

This circle of friends is the circle of life.
May this gift both soothe and delight
so that the goddess we call does indeed
shine her light to bless all here in
friendship that forever burns bright.

DECEMBER 2024

NOTES	SUNDAY	MONDAY	TUESDAY
	● 1	2	3
	WORLD AIDS DAY		INTERNATIONAL DAY OF PERSONS WITH DISABILITIES
	◐ 8	9	10
			HUMAN RIGHTS DAY
	○ 15	16	17
	◐ 22	23	24
			CHRISTMAS EVE
	29	● 30	31
			NEW YEAR'S EVE

DECEMBER 2024

WEDNESDAY	THURSDAY	FRIDAY	SATURDAY
4	5	6	7
11	12	13	14
18	19	20	21 WINTER SOLSTICE
25 CHRISTMAS DAY HANUKKAH (BEGINS AT SUNDOWN)	26 BOXING DAY (UK / CAN / AUS / NZ) FIRST DAY OF KWANZAA	27	28

HEMATITE

Hematite is an iron oxide, usually formed in the presence of water, and among the most abundant minerals on Earth. Although steely gray to black, and sometimes red, in color, it produces reddish streaks when tested and in its abundance on Mars is credited for the planet's nickname: the red planet. Appropriately, hematite derives from *haimatitis*, Greek for "blood red," which is hematite's color when ground into a powder. It is a deeply grounding stone that provides ease and confidence.

 Magical force: Hematite is the stone of the mind and encourages learning, focus, and deep thought; it releases practical wisdom and boosts self-confidence. Let hematite protect you, as well, from harmful energies meant to attack: placed in the corners of your home, or a specific room, hematite emits a protective shield while absorbing the harmful energy. Hematite can be useful in both scrying and meditation work by clearing away the cobwebs and revealing the truth that needs to be seen.

 Chakra correspondence: *Root*—grounds energy flow deeply connected to Earth.

November / December

MONDAY (NOVEMBER)
25

TUESDAY (NOVEMBER)
26

WEDNESDAY (NOVEMBER)
27

THURSDAY (NOVEMBER) THANKSGIVING DAY (US)
28

FRIDAY (NOVEMBER) NATIVE AMERICAN HERITAGE DAY (US)
29

SATURDAY (NOVEMBER)
30

SUNDAY WORLD AIDS DAY ●
1

December 2024

MONDAY

2

TUESDAY INTERNATIONAL DAY OF PERSONS WITH DISABILITIES

3

WEDNESDAY

4

THURSDAY

5

FRIDAY

6

SATURDAY

7

SUNDAY

8

MALACHITE

Working with malachite allows our subconscious to reveal what we need and grasp what our emotions are trying to tell us. It instills leadership and the confidence to take action for change.

December 2024

MONDAY

9

TUESDAY HUMAN RIGHTS DAY

10

WEDNESDAY

11

THURSDAY

12

FRIDAY 13

SATURDAY 14

SUNDAY ○ 15

With humble heart, I vow to see the truth of my mistakes. With human heart, I show myself forgiving, healing grace. With loving heart, forgiveness means that love will take pain's place.

December 2024

MONDAY   16

TUESDAY   17

WEDNESDAY   18

THURSDAY   19

FRIDAY

20

SATURDAY WINTER SOLSTICE

21

SUNDAY

22

There is no limit to what the Universe provides. I am grateful for all I have and worthy of all I achieve. Choices are abundant: I choose success.

December 2024

MONDAY

23

TUESDAY CHRISTMAS EVE

24

WEDNESDAY CHRISTMAS DAY / HANUKKAH (BEGINS AT SUNDOWN)

25

THURSDAY BOXING DAY (UK / CAN / AUS / NZ) / FIRST DAY OF KWANZAA

26

FRIDAY

27

SATURDAY

28

SUNDAY

29

Trust that what's meant for you will
manifest at the time you need it most.

December 2024

MONDAY ●

30

TUESDAY <small>NEW YEAR'S EVE</small>

31

WEDNESDAY (JANUARY) <small>NEW YEAR'S DAY</small>

1

THURSDAY (JANUARY)

2

NOTES

NOTES

NOTES

NOTES

NOTES

Inspiring | Educating | Creating | Entertaining

Brimming with creative inspiration, how-to projects, and useful information to enrich your everyday life, quarto.com is a favorite destination for those pursuing their interests and passions.

First published in 2023 by Rock Point,
an imprint of The Quarto Group
142 West 36th Street, 4th Floor
New York, NY 10018, USA
T (212) 779-4972 F (212) 779-6058
www.Quarto.com

Contains content previously published in 2022 as *Crystal Magic*, *Love Spells*, and *Protection Spells* by Wellfleet Press, an imprint of The Quarto Group, 142 West 36th Street, 4th Floor, New York, NY 10018.

Rock Point titles are also available at discount for retail, wholesale, promotional, and bulk purchase. For details, contact the Special Sales Manager by email at specialsales@quarto.com or by mail at The Quarto Group, Attn: Special Sales Manager, 100 Cummings Center Suite 265D, Beverly, MA 01915 USA.

10 9 8 7 6 5 4 3 2 1

ISBN: 978-1-63106-954-3

Publisher: Rage Kindelsperger
Creative Director: Laura Drew
Managing Editor: Cara Donaldson
Editor: Sara Bonacum
Editorial Assistant: Katelynn Abraham
Interior Design: Laura Klynstra
Layout Design: Carlos Esparza

Printed in China

This planner provides general information on various widely known and widely accepted self-care practices. However, it should not be relied upon as recommending or promoting any specific diagnosis or method of treatment for a particular condition, and it is not intended as a substitute for medical advice or for direct diagnosis and treatment of a medical condition by a qualified physician. Readers who have questions about a particular condition, possible treatments for that condition, or possible reactions from the condition or its treatment should consult a physician or other qualified healthcare professional.

All Moon phases shown are for the Eastern Time Zone.